A Happy Old Age

Dr. Ashton Oxenden (1808-1892)

A Happy Old Age

Ashton Oxenden

Edited by Joel R. Beeke

REFORMATION HERITAGE BOOKS
Grand Rapids, Michigan

Copyright © 2004
Reformation Heritage Books
2965 Leonard St., NE, Grand Rapids, Michigan 49525
Phone: 616-977-0599 / Fax: 616-285-3246
e-mail: orders@heritagebooks.org
website: www.heritagebooks.org

ISBN #978-1-892777-32-4
Second printing 2012

Foreword

A Happy Old Age was written by Dr. Ashton Oxenden, Anglican Bishop of Montreal and Metropolitan of Canada in the nineteenth century. In twelve short chapters the book provides simple, heartfelt, spiritual advice to the elderly on important issues and topics, such as the duties, temptations, trials, and joys of old age. The author's aim is to lead his readers to true happiness in the Lord Jesus Christ, and to show how to live actively and fruitfully in Christian service in the final years of one's life (Psalm 92:12-15).

Ashton Oxenden (1808-1892) was born at Broome Park, Canterbury, England. He was the fifth son of Sir Henry Oxenden and Mary Graham, daughter of Colonel Graham of St. Lawrence. Sir Henry Oxenden educated his son privately for several years, then sent him to schools in Ramsgate and Harrow. In 1827, Ashton entered University College, Oxford, graduating four years later with a Bachelor of Arts degree.

Oxenden was ordained in Lambeth in 1833. He served as curate in Barham, Kent for five years, then resigned because of ill health; he did not fully recover for seven or eight years.

From 1849 to 1869 Oxenden served as vicar of Pluckley. At Pluckley he began to preach extemporaneously. He also wrote his Barham tracts during this time. Oxenden did not marry until the age of fifty-six, after briefly courting Sarah Bradshaw. They had one child, Mary Ashton Oxenden, who later married Sir David Wood, gentleman in waiting to Princess Fredrica of Hanover, daughter of the King of Hanover.

During the 1860s, Oxenden traveled around the world. He became Bishop of Montreal and

Metropolitan of Canada in 1869. Most of Montreal's inhabitants were Roman Catholics, but the Church of England in Canada (since 1955, the Anglican Church of Canada) had twelve churches in Montreal. As Bishop he had charge of these twelve churches; as Metropolitan of Canada he was the "bishop of bishops," outranking all the others, having the status of an archbishop. He worked hard, ministering during winters in Montreal and spending summers visiting the country districts. Poor health compelled him to resign his offices at the age of seventy.

Oxenden then returned to England. In 1879, he accepted a call to serve as vicar of St. Stephen's and as rural dean of Canterbury. In 1885, ill health once more compelled him to quit the ministry. In his autobiography, *The History of My Life* (London: Longmans, Green and Co., 1891), Oxenden wrote, "I was called upon to bid another farewell, and to burst the bonds which bound me so strongly to this my last and very dear flock." Oxenden retired to Biarritz where he died at age eighty-four on February 22, 1892.

Oxenden wrote at least forty-five books. Nearly all of his writings were popular due to their simple style and practical content. His style of writing is similar to that of his contemporary and fellow bishop, J. C. Ryle (1816-1900). Oxenden's *Pathway of Safety* sold 350,000 copies and his *Christian Life* sold 47,000 copies. His Barham tracts, published as *Cottage Readings* in 1859, were very popular. Other influential titles included *The Cottage Library* (six volumes), *Family Prayers, The Fourfold Picture of the Sinner, Sermons on the Christian Life, Words of Peace, The Parables of Our Lord Explained, A Plain History of the Christian Church, A Simple Exposition of the Psalms, Counsel to the Confirmed, Touchstone: Christian Graces and Characters*

Tested, Plain Sermons, Baptism Simply Explained, The Earnest Communicant, and *The Pastoral Office.*

A Happy Old Age was first printed as *The Home Beyond; or, A Happy Old Age* in 1861 (10,000 copies), then reprinted several times in the late nineteenth century. Editing in this new printing has been minimal. Obsolete words have been updated; punctuation and spelling have been modernized. We have enlarged the type size of this little book to accommodate readers who prefer a larger font.

Oxenden's advice applies to all ages. Have you been taught to number your days so that you may apply your heart unto wisdom? Have you counted today as one more day closer to being with the Lord? To answer these questions rightly, you must know the Lord Jesus Christ who is Wisdom itself as your Savior, your love, your life, your all in all (Col. 3:11). Then your only comfort in life and death is that you are not your own, but belong unto your faithful Savior Jesus Christ who makes you willing and ready to live unto Him (cf. Heidelberg Catechism, Q. 1).

If you cannot say yes to those questions, we advise you to make haste to repent and believe the gospel for your life's sake. You have only a short time left, no matter what your age, and if you waste your life by not fleeing to Christ in repentance and faith, you will have to suffer the consequences of being forever separated from God's favor (cf. John 3:36).

Read this book prayerfully that you may grow in grace, or, if you are yet unsaved, cry out, "Lord, save me, or I perish." May this book help prepare you to finish your course in a God-glorifying way and to see by faith what awaits you on the other side in the home beyond.

—Joel and John Beeke

CONTENTS

~1~

Life's Journey

What is our life? It is a journey that is soon ended; a tale that is quickly told; a day, whose hours roll by apace. It is a vapor, which rises for a while, and then vanishes; a flame that burns for a moment or two, and then flickers in the socket, and presently goes out. Our little lifetime, oh, how short it is!

And what are your thoughts, my aged friend, about this journey of life? Once you looked upon it as a very different thing from what it appears to you now. Once it seemed to you as if the days of your childhood would never pass away. You longed for manhood or womanhood, but it came very slowly. The early stages of your journey seemed almost endless. And if it had been possible, you would willingly have taken a spring, and jumped into middle life with a bound. But now you look back, and wonder how quickly your life has passed. It seems but yesterday you were a child. Old age has crept in, almost without your knowing it.

Truly the longest life is but a little while, when

compared with eternity. It is but a tiny drop in the wide ocean, but as a grain of sand on the boundless shore, "so soon passeth it away, and we are gone." And when we look forward, how soon shall we be in our graves! A few more days and we shall come to the end of our span. Very soon "the silver cord" will be "loosed," "the golden bowl" will be "broken," "the pitcher" will be fairly worn out, "the wheel" will make its last turn; and then we shall "go to our long home, and the mourners go about the streets" (Eccl. 7:5-6).

I want you to open your Bible, and turn to the ninetieth Psalm. Take it, and ponder it over in your heart; and I think you will find it very profitable sometimes to *use it as a prayer for yourself.* The writer of that Psalm must, I think, have been an old man; and he must have written it on purpose for those of his brethren who are going down the hill of life.

I once heard of an aged Christian who used to be very fond of applying the ninety-first Psalm to himself. He loved to think how truly it set forth the faithfulness of God to him during his long life. When he was on his deathbed, he exclaimed, in the words of the last verse: "With long life has He satisfied me, and now I am going to enjoy the only portion which I could not have in this life—He is going to *show me His salvation.*"

Perhaps, dear reader, you are drawing to the close of a long life. It may be that your thoughts have long been turned heavenwards. And if so,

I know that a word of counsel will be welcome to you. But if, on the other hand, you have been thoughtless hitherto, I will try and make you thoughtful now. Whatever has been your past history, I want to give you a few hints in this book as to how you may turn to the best account the time that still remains to you. I want to do you some good. I want to make your last days the best and happiest of all your life.

I observe that old persons are in some respects much alike, but are in other respects very different.

They are *alike* in their infirmities. Their limbs shake and totter. Their bodies have grown weak. The clay house they dwell in is the worse for wear. Their minds, too, have lost their former strength. Memory fails them. They can recollect what happened years and years ago, but what happened yesterday is gone—all is as a blank.

They are also *alike* in their sorrows. They have known what affliction is. Some have had to mourn over thoughtless, undutiful, and rebellious children. Some have had to weep over many an open grave. Some have found from sad experience that the world is but a sorry house to live in. In these respects old people are much alike.

But in other respects, how *different* they are! Some are rich, while others are poor. Some have but few cares and troubles in their declining years, while others are burdened with anxieties. Some again have many friends around them, who show them kindness, while others are left alone with no one to care for them.

But there is *a still greater difference* between those who are far advanced in years. Here is one stooping and groaning under his heavy burden, vexed with all around him, full of complainings, discontented with his lot, having no pleasure in life, and yet clinging to it as a drowning man grasps at the only plank that is left—tired of this world, and yet having no hope beyond it.

We see another with the same gray head and the same bent body; but there is a beam that lights up his aged countenance. He is thankful, contented, peaceful. All goes well with him. He is willing, cheerfully willing, to bear all that God lays upon him. Not a murmur escapes his lips, not a distrustful feeling dwells within. There is a calm tide of joy flowing through his soul.

How is this? What makes all this difference? It is God's grace alone. This fills the heart with peace. This gives comfort and rest now, and awakens in the soul a sweet and blessed hope of joys to come.

Such an old age as this is most desirable, is it not? And such an old age, dear reader, is just what I desire for *you*. May it be *your* portion.

I once heard of an old man who was brought to God late in life. He desired that, when he died, these words might be written on his tombstone: "Here lies an old man of *seven* years of age."

And why so? The truth was, that all the past

years of his long life he counted as no life at all, for his soul was dead. It was only during the last few years that he had *really* lived, for he had then lived to God.

You are now grown old. The shades of evening are growing thick around you. You are come to the last stage of life's journey. Your state is something like that of Moses, when he had traveled for forty years through the wilderness, and was now come to his journey's end. The Lord announces to him that his death is near. But before he departs, He bids him go up to the top of Pisgah. There he was able to look back on the path along which he had been brought, and look forward to the Land of Promise.

It must have been very good for him to take a survey of that winding path along which God had led him; to cast his eye back upon the many spots where mercy had been shown him; to call to mind all the difficulties and dangers he had passed through, and the gracious manner in which his God had borne with him, notwithstanding his many sins.

Now, this is just the survey which you should take, my aged friend. Get a quiet half-hour now and then, and look back into the past. It will be good for you, I am sure, and I counsel you to try it. I will help you to do so in the next chapter.

~2~

The Days That Are Past

You remember that I spoke in my last chapter of what Moses did before he died. He was directed to go up on Mount Pisgah, and take a glimpse of that Promised Land which lay before him. But we can hardly imagine that this was all he did. It is more than likely that another purpose for which he ascended that high hill was that he might from thence take a survey of all the way that he had *already* traveled in his wilderness journey. I said that it would be well for you now and then to look back on all the years that you have passed through. Let me now help you a little in doing this.

First, take a good searching look, and see *what sins have marked your past life*. And as you look back, you will feel, I dare say, that there is many an act which you would gladly blot out if you could. There are many days you would like to live over again in the hope that you would live them better; many words you would like to recall; many a deed which you would give worlds to undo; many a bad thought which you encouraged, and which has left a stain behind that even time cannot wear out.

I know it is very painful to be thinking about our past sins, but we must not shrink from it. It is folly to deceive ourselves, and imagine that they have not been committed. There they are, and God sees them, if we will not. His eye marked them at the time, and it marks them still. They may almost have faded away from our memory; but God remembers them: He forgets nothing.

Old people are very apt to think that what is past and forgotten by them is also blotted out of the book of God's remembrance. Often, for instance, when the sins and follies of their youth are spoken of, they just heave a passing sigh, and that is all. They think that such things are excusable in times of youth, and that God will not be extreme to mark what was done amiss in those days. They fancy that the distant past will not be laid to their charge, as they have since become wiser and more thoughtful.

But is it so? Is God such an one as ourselves? Can any length of time wear away our sins from His recollection? Is it not written that even "for every *idle word* that men shall speak they must give an account?"

I am sure it is very good for us all, and especially for those who are drawing near to the close of life, to look fairly at the sins that we have committed. It is folly to close our eyes to them and persuade ourselves they do not exist. Indeed, if we have any spiritual life in us, whatever else we forget, surely we shall never forget those hateful sins which have defiled our souls.

But it is not enough to look at them in a *general way*. We must fix upon them *one by one*, and draw them forth from their hiding-places. There must be a close searching for them, as with a candle—an honest, hearty, diligent search, so that not one shall escape us.

"And what is the good of this?" you are perhaps ready to ask. "Is there any use in making ourselves unhappy? The thing is done; can it be undone?"

Oh, surely it is far better to discover our sins now, than to have them brought to light for the first time when we appear before God. It is far better to know how we stand with God now than to learn it in that world where there is no more hope for the sinner.

And *what are we to do with our sins* when we have found them out? Is there any way by which they can be got rid of? Or must they lie like dark spots on our souls, like unpaid debts, which can never be cancelled? No, dear friend, no. There is a way, one way only, by which every sin committed and every deed left undone can be blotted out for ever. Christ has paid the debt for sinners. He has bled for sinners like you on the cross. He has died that sinners might live. And He is able, at this moment, not only to pardon your every sin, but to cover you with His perfect righteousness, and to make you His forever; "he is able also to save them to the uttermost that come unto God by him" (Heb. 7:25).

Go now to Jesus, and ask Him to give you repentance (Acts 5:31). Ask Him by His Holy Spirit to touch your heart, and to make you hate your sins and mourn over them with godly sorrow. Oh, it is good for us to feel grief for our sins. And depend upon it; we *shall* grieve over them, if we are brought under the power of God's grace.

But remember, sorrow and tears will not wash out the stain. They cannot remove one single atom of our guilt. No, only the sacrifice of Christ can pay that debt. In Him alone forgiveness can be found. "The blood of Jesus Christ his Son cleanseth us from all sin" (1 John 1:7).

Here then, my dear friend, is the good of finding out our many sins. It is that we may get every one of them pardoned; it is that we may be made happy in Christ our Savior. He is all power and love. He is able and willing to save. He says, "Come unto me...and I will give you rest"; "Though your sins be as scarlet, they shall be as white as snow; though they be red like crimson, they shall be as wool" (Matt. 11:28; Isa. 1:18).

But there is something more we should look back upon, besides our sins; we should look back upon *our many mercies* (Ps. 103:1-5).

Think of the numberless acts of love and kindness which God has shown you during the years that are past. Moses called to mind, I dare say, those forty years in which the Lord had so greatly blessed him. The whole path which he had trodden was indeed strewn with mercies—mercies to himself, to his family, to his people. We are told that for forty years their "raiment waxed not old, neither did [their] feet swell" (Deut. 8:4). When they were thirsty, "He brought streams also out of the rock, and caused waters to run down like rivers" (Ps. 78:16). When they were hungry, He fed them with bread from heaven (Ex. 16:4). He led them, not by the shortest road nor by the easiest path, but it was "by the right way," to their promised land.

Has not the Lord dealt as graciously with you? Have not goodness and mercy followed you all your days? Think of your many deliverances from dangers. Think how you have been spared, while others have been cut off. Think of all the blessings which came to you when you deserved them so little. Think of God's patience with you when you provoked His anger. Think how He made one thing and another work for your good. Many a time you said within yourself, "This thing is unfortunate; it is all against me"; and perhaps that very thing turned out to be for your greatest good.

God's past mercies should be a pledge to you of those that are to come. You may well plead with David, "O God, thou hast taught me from my youth...now also when I am old and gray-headed, O God, forsake me not" (Ps. 71:17-18). You may expect further trials as you reach the remaining stages of the wilderness. But you may be sure that the manna with which you have been fed will not fail, nor the cloud of protection which has sheltered you be withdrawn, until your wanderings are over. Be assured, God never yet forsook a worn-out pilgrim. He never yet neglected an aged servant. You know that He has promised you, "Even to your old age, I am he; and even to hoar hairs, I will carry you. I have made, and I will bear; even I will carry and deliver you" (Isa. 46:4). The last words of good old Dr. Guyse were, "O my God! Thou hast always been with me, and wilt not leave me *now*."

Think of all this, and it will warm your cold heart. You will find some love kindling within you as you call to mind the goodness of that heavenly Friend who has watched over you so lovingly, and cared for you from your childhood until now.

And oh, if you are a true servant of God, if you have been brought to know and love your Savior, if the path of godliness has been your path, then is there not one mercy which exceeds every other in your case? Does not your heart throb with gratitude when you think of that grace which called you out of darkness into the blessed light of God's truth, which turned your feet out of the path of sin and misery along which you were then hurrying, and brought you into the way of peace?

Of all your mercies, there is none so great as that which led you to Christ and made you a partaker of His great salvation.

It is said of John Newton that although his memory failed him in his old age, there were two things which he never forgot: one was that "he was a *great sinner*"; and the other was that "Jesus was a *greater Savior*."

Let me urge you then to take both a look back on *your past sins* and on *your past mercies*. This is especially needful for you who have lived many years in this world and whose hourglass has but a few grains yet to run out. Do so in a humble and thoughtful spirit, and I believe you will find that much good will come from it.

Take this and any other counsels which I offer you, as coming from one who really cares for you. Yes, I feel for the aged. I know their trials, their infirmities, and their difficulties. But I also know that the Savior Himself cares for you. He has in store many and great blessings, which He is quite ready to bestow upon you. And what I desire, in this book, is to lead you to the enjoyment of them, so that yours may be a blessed and happy old age.

The Duties of Old Age

Every station and stage of life has its own special duties. Childhood has its duties, such as obedience to parents, modesty, and willingness to be taught. A husband and wife have their duties. Manhood has its duties; grown-up men or women are required to be useful in the world, and not to live unto themselves, but unto the Lord.

And so, too, old age has its duties. I will mention some of them.

1. You should endeavor to be *patient and gentle*. Amid all your pains and infirmities, how blessed if you can feel a cheerful submission to God's will, and if you can accept, not merely with resignation, but with actual thankfulness, all that He lays upon you. God can give you this patient, humble, submissive spirit if you will earnestly and daily seek it from Him.

2. You should try to be *cheerful and considerate of others*. Sometimes old people are a little apt to dwell too much on their own troubles and de-

sires. Guard against this, and seek to make those around you happy. You cannot do much, perhaps, but you can do something. A gentle word or two, or even a kind look, will cheer some and encourage others.

Little drops of water, little grains of sand,
Make the boundless ocean, and the beauteous land;
Little deeds of kindness, little words of love,
Make our earth an Eden, like the heaven above.

Do not grudge young people those delights which you can no longer enjoy. But put yourself often in their place, and remember that you were once a child yourself. The very fact that you are trying to make others happy will make you happy yourself.

3. Be much in *prayer* and in the *reading of God's Word*. These are great helps to a Christian pilgrim; they are like so many staffs by the way. Use them diligently and they will help you onward. As you read a little further, you will find some directions how to profit by the use of them.

4. You should *sit loose to this world*, and be in readiness to leave it. This, you will say, is the duty of us all. Yes, but it is especially your duty; for the clock of time seems now to be sounding its warning-alarm in your ears. Every day seems to be saying to you, "Prepare to meet thy God!

The night is far spent; the day is at hand. The judge standeth at the door."

It is a sad sight to see an old person bent down with years, standing at the edge of eternity, and yet unwilling to loose his hold of this world—clinging to life with an eager grasp, as much busied as ever with its trifling concerns, still thirsting for its poor pleasures and yet unable to enjoy them, all before him a blank, having no hope as regards the future. Such an old age is indeed a sad one.

But you will perhaps say, "Surely when any one has grown old, and when he has sown the wild oats of youth, he will, as a matter of course, become thoughtful, and turn his mind towards that world he is so shortly to enter." But no; this does not at all follow. On the contrary, I have seen many in old age be just as worldly-minded as ever, putting from them, even then, the thoughts of a life to come.

Dear friend, only grace can make you anxious about your soul. Only grace can prepare you for eternity. We all need the powerful working of God's Spirit to draw our minds from earth to heaven, from sin to holiness.

Happy for you, if heaven is the home of your heart! Happy for you, if your thoughts are centered there! Happy for you, if you can say, "The world is crucified unto me, and I unto the world" (Gal. 6:14b); "we look not at the things which

are seen, but at the things which are not seen"
(2 Cor. 4:18).

5. *Your conversation should be heavenly.* Your time
is nearly ended; therefore, you should not think
much about this world which you are about to
leave. Its pleasures, its riches, its occupations
should not occupy your mind. You should rather
busy yourself with preparations for your journey
to your everlasting home. You should love to
speak about your Father's house.

True, our evil hearts will ever be "cleaving to
the dust" (Ps. 119:25). There is a weight upon
our wings ever keeping us downwards. But oh,
struggle against this. Pray against it. Ask God to
be continually drawing your mind heavenward,
and to enable you to "set your affections on
things above" (Col. 3:2). Speak thankfully of His
preserving mercy. Bear testimony to His goodness and faithfulness, and recommend others
to trust Him without a doubt, and to give their
whole hearts to Him.

6. Try to set a *good example for others.* We should
all wish to be useful in the world. But now that
you are grown old, you feel perhaps that your
time for usefulness is past. Satan may whisper,
"You are too old to be useful now." But not so;
you may do something still. It is true you cannot
labor for your family as you once did. You cannot go here and there to help those who need

your assistance. But you may be very useful even now—useful if you are rich, and useful, too, if you are poor. As you sit by your fireside, you may speak Christian words; you may show by your conduct and temper the blessed effects that religion has upon your heart. You may, by your prayers and praises, by your patience and perseverance, by your watching and waiting, glorify God. A truly Christian old man or woman may thus be a great blessing to the house and place in which he is living. He may spread a feeling of contentment around him. He may stop many a bad work, and soften many a quarrelsome spirit. He may show forth so clearly the power of grace in his own conduct that he may lead others to seek it, and pray for it themselves.

Without *speaking* much, or *doing* much, you may honor God by your Christian *conduct*; and thus your light may so shine before men, that you may glorify Him. We know that a nice picture in a room is a pleasant thing to gaze upon; we constantly turn to it with pleasure. And what picture is there more beautiful than that of an aged Christian, old in years, and ripe in grace? "The hoary head is a crown of glory, if it be found in the way of righteousness" (Prov. 16:31).

Yes, remember always you may do much by your example. This will say more than your words, for your words may be mistaken, but your life cannot be. It must and will speak. Paul reminded the Corinthians of this when he said,

"Ye are our epistle...*known and read of all men*: Forasmuch as ye are manifestly declared to be the epistle of Christ" (2 Cor. 3:2-3); that is, your lives plainly declare whose and what you are.

These are some of the duties which belong to old people. Dear reader, neglect them not; try to fulfill them. It will be for your own happiness, and for the good of others. Thus you will be "bearing fruit in old age."

~4~

The Temptations of
Old Age

Satan tempts every one of us. Who is there that has not felt his power? And oh, how craftily does he apply his temptations! He suits them exactly to our stations and ages. He has some temptations for the rich, others for the poor; some for the young, and others for the old. He knows our weak points, and there he assaults us.

So you must not be surprised if you have your temptations, and perhaps sore ones, too. You may be one of God's dearest children, and yet be tempted. Was not Joseph tempted, and David, and Paul? And was not even Jesus, the sinless Savior, tempted by Satan?

Never be angry with yourself because you are thus tried. It is no sin to be tempted. It is only when we *give way to temptation*, instead of resisting it, that God is angry with us. It is the falling into sin that grieves and offends Him.

When you find yourself tempted to any wrong feeling, or to do anything sinful, I will tell you

how to act. Don't give yourself up to the temptation, but strive resolutely against it. And as you
have but little strength of your own, fly unto God
for help. Turn at once to Him. Satan is strong,
but there is a stronger One than he. Jesus knows
both Satan's power and your weakness; and,
as "he himself hath suffered being tempted, he
is able to succor them that are tempted" (Heb.
2:18). In Christ you are safe, and nowhere else.
He can throw His shelter around you, and protect
you from all harm.

But let us see what kinds of temptation belong especially to the aged.

A *deadness and dullness of soul* is very apt to come
over an old person. Your feelings are not so lively
and strong as they once were. Your affections are
somewhat blunted. There was a time when a powerful sermon or a striking book moved you, and
tears filled your eyes. The love of Jesus made your
heart glow. But perhaps this warmth and tenderness of spirit is, in a measure, gone.

Now, you have need to be on your guard on
this point. Take care that you do not settle down
into a cold and easy frame of mind. Take care that
your faith does not wither, and your love grow
dull. It will do so if you are not very watchful.
Pray constantly that God may touch your heart,
and give life to it. Especially pray that you may
have a bright view of that gracious Savior, who
has done so much for you.

Very often, too, seniors give way to a *peevish and irritable temper.* They allow little things to ruffle them. This is wrong, and it very much interferes with their happiness.

When you yourself have indulged in this spirit, what has been the consequence? Why, you have felt thoroughly uncomfortable afterwards, and you have wished that you had more command over yourself.

Watch against it then. I know that it is one of the temptations to which old age is especially liable. But God can strengthen you against it. He can enable you to overcome it instead of it overcoming you. He can give you a happy, contented, peaceful frame of mind, and enable you to take all the little rough edges of life with calmness and evenness of temper. Thus will your latter days be happy, instead of miserable; and you will enjoy a peace within, of which nothing can rob you.

Again there is such a thing as *weariness of life,* which is very wrong to encourage. At the end of sixty or seventy years, a person often feels a little tired of this world. He is weary of its trials. He has tasted of its disappointments. He wishes to get away from them. A suffering body, too, perhaps weighs him down. And he is ready to cry out with David, "Oh, that I had wings like a dove! for then would I fly away, and be at rest" (Ps. 55:6).

But this is not a right wish. We ought cheerfully to bear all that our heavenly Father sees good for us to bear. Even our greatest sufferings should be willingly endured for His sake. Christ could say in the very midst of His agony, "The cup which my Father hath given me, shall I not drink it?" (John 18:11). Elijah was wrong when he requested for himself that he might die, and said, "Now, O Lord, take away my life" (1 Kings 19:4). Jonah, too, was wrong when he exclaimed, "It is better for me to die than to live" (Jonah 4:3). There was a good deal of discontentment in the minds of all these persons when they made such a request. It was in a moment of disappointment and distrust that they breathed such prayers.

How different were Paul's feelings when he expressed a "desire to depart" (Phil. 1:23). It was not because he was tired of life, nor because he was discontented with the lot which God had appointed for him. No; he desired to depart for a far different reason. It was because he wished to be with Christ. He loved his Savior, and longed to be in His presence.

May God give us the same holy longing, and may we at the same time be content to remain here just so long as He in His wisdom and love sees fit.

My dear friend, you see there are certain temptations to which in your old age you are especially liable. I have mentioned three—namely, deadness of soul, peevishness, and unwillingness to bear the sufferings of this life. But there are others which I have not mentioned. Now, look well into your heart, and think what is the temptation to which you are most inclined to yield. And then ask God to set you free from it, and to strengthen you by putting His Holy Spirit within your heart. That was a comforting word which our Lord spoke to Peter, "Satan hath desired to have you, that he may sift you as wheat; *but I have prayed for thee*, that thy faith fail not" (Luke 22:31-32).

Satan is a *mighty* tempter, but you have an *almighty* Protector. Rest in His promise. Trust in His strength, and no power on earth or in hell can ever harm you.

~5~

The Trials of Old Age

This life is a life of trials; who is there altogether free from them? We must expect them, and be ready to meet them when they come. Sometimes they cluster so thickly around us that we need a stout heart and much grace to bear them meekly, and to pass through them unhurt.

Let us talk about those trials that belong to old age; perhaps we shall find ourselves all the better for saying a few words about them.

Loss of strength is a great trial to an old person. It is painful to feel that you cannot do many things now which you once did so easily. To be busy and happy was once perhaps your greatest enjoyment. But now your limbs can hardly carry you; many of the occupations of life are a burden to you.

But let not this distress you. It is your portion, and God has so ordered it. Though the "outer man perish," He can strengthen you in your soul, so that the "inner man is renewed day by day" (2 Cor. 4:16).

And is there not mercy in your very feebleness? It reminds you constantly that your life is drawing to a close, while a voice from heaven whispers to you that "there remaineth therefore a rest to the people of God" (Heb. 4:9). In that heavenly home there will be no weakness, no weariness, no infirmity, and no sin.

Loss of memory is another great trial that generally accompanies old age. I imagine you can remember pretty well what happened years ago; but you entirely forget what happened yesterday. What you read is soon lost; it passes away like letters written on the sand. You hear a sermon, and what your minister said is all gone an hour later; even the very text is forgotten. You may sometimes be vexed with yourself for this, and you even fear that God may be angry with you. But no; He is no hard master. He does not reap where He has not sown (Luke 19:21). He is quite aware of your infirmities. He knows very well the weakness of your frame, and remembers that you are but dust (Ps. 103:14). He is too kind and too just to require of you what you cannot give Him.

Never mind then the weakness of your memory. God will not call you to account for that. The great thing is to have your heart right with God. Entreat Him to cleanse and purify your heart by His Holy Spirit, and then all will be well.

There is a third loss which old persons often mourn over, and that is the *loss of friends*. One after another dies, and they find themselves left behind like a solitary tree in the wilderness. Their dearest children have perhaps been taken from them; maybe a lonely widowhood is their portion. There is something sad in all this. It is sad indeed to see an aged one bereft of those who once clung to him with fond affection, and now left all alone. But, my dear friend, remember this: you will never be alone if God is your God. Christ is the Friend, the Brother, the Husband of His people. Others may forsake you, but He never will. You may reckon on His love; it will not fail you. He is with you now, and He will never leave nor forsake you. If you can say, "The Lord is my Shepherd," then you may add, "therefore I shall not want."

Old people often feel also that they are only *a trouble to others*. This is a heavy trial to some. But why should it be? It is the will of God that we should look to others for help in infancy and old age. Surely a son or a daughter ought to feel it not only a sacred duty, but also a pleasure, to supply the needs of an aged parent. And I am sure, where the heart is right, it will be done with real cheerfulness and goodwill.

There is one more trial which I will mention—the feeling of *not being able to earn one's own livelihood.* If a person has honestly supported himself and his family during a long life, he does not like to feel that he must be beholden to others in his latter days. Perhaps this is the case with you. Perhaps you laid aside some money in younger days, and looked forward to maintaining yourself in old age. But you lent your money to a friend, and he has made off with it; or you had a long illness, and all your savings were spent during that time; and now you are forced to depend on the kindness of friends, or church support.

Well, if such be the case, you have no cause to blame yourself, and there is no disgrace whatever in being financially dependent on others. Instead of feeling such, you may well be thankful that there are ways in which you can be helped in the hour of your need. Look upon those who assist you as sent by your heavenly Father. He graciously provides means for supplying your necessities. He raises you up friends; He puts it into their hearts to help you. He is the great Fountain from whence all your blessings flow.

Receive then every gift as from God. Acknowledge His hand in it, and depend on Him from day to day for all you need. I believe that if we thus trust God we shall never be disappointed. We may sometimes be driven hard. There may be but a little meal in our barrel, and but a few drops of oil in our cruse; but let us remember that word which comforted Abraham of old—"Jehovah-jireh," *The Lord will provide.* He who feeds the ravens will feed you. He cares for His people, and will never let them lack. "I have been young," said David, "and now am old; yet have I not seen the righteous forsaken, nor his seed begging bread" (Ps. 37:25).

I have mentioned some of your trials. And I dare say there are many more, many which the world knows nothing about, and which none will ever know but yourself. But however thick they fall around you, and however heavily they press upon you, you have only to carry them to God and He will lighten your load and make it easy to bear. Here is your remedy, and a promise with it: "Cast thy burden upon the Lord, and he shall sustain thee" (Ps. 55:22). He will not only *carry your burdens*, but He will *carry you*. He who has so often laid you as a lamb in His bosom will carry you now that you are old. He will never turn away from you, but rejoice over you and do you good. He will be with you amid all your infirmities. He will not only bring you to Jordan, but will carry you over it, and conduct you safely into the Promised Land.

And then, too, remember that your trials are good for you. If we had none, we should be like bullocks unaccustomed to the yoke; we should have our own way too much, and never learn submission to our Father's will. Our Lord suffered, and shall not we? It was His daily portion when on earth; let us not wish to escape it.

As it is, we are tied and bound to this world far too much. We love it too well. How would it be if we met with no trials here? We should be still less disposed than we are now to look for another resting place above.

Think, too, how light our trials are, compared with the Savior's. His was a storm of suffering; ours but a few drops. And for how short a time do our troubles last, even the severest of them! They are "but for a moment." In eternity, how small they will seem to us as we look back upon them! In heaven, we shall thank God for them, for we shall then see how necessary they were for us.

Cheer up then, my fellow-Christian. Bear these trials of yours patiently, meekly, and thankfully. Look on them as the sick man looks on the remedies which are sent to do him good. Look on them as the traveller looks on the rough rocks which serve as steps to bring him to his father's house.

Turn your trials to good account. Let them not be hindrances to you, but helps, on your way to heaven. Ask God to change them into blessings, and to make them useful to you. Just as, when Noah was in the ark, every wave that swelled only bore him up higher and higher towards heaven, so may every trial raise your soul above the world, and bring you nearer and nearer to God!

6

The Joys of Old Age

A happy old age! Is such a thing possible? Do we ever meet with an old, worn out person who is really happy? Is the evening of life ever bright and sunny? Yes, such a thing is quite possible; we meet with it now and then. Though the body is decayed by time, the limbs are feeble, and the mind is somewhat weakened, yet there still may be a calm joy within, a peace which time can never wear out.

Dear brother or sister, do *you* wish to be happy? I know you do; everyone is a seeker after happiness, though many look for it in the wrong direction, and therefore never find it.

Shall I tell you how and where to find happiness? The *world* cannot give it to you. It holds out large promises, but it has no peace to bestow. *Friends* cannot give it to you. It is a blessing to have kind friends, and to be surrounded by those who love us; but this cannot give peace to the conscience. *Money* cannot give it to you. It is well to have enough, and something to spare. I dare say you often long to be a little richer than you now are. But money cannot drive away care or bring joy to the heart.

What is it then that will make us *truly happy?* The grace of God is the one great thing which can bring peace to the soul. Oh, what a happiness to know that He is your Father and your Friend! To be able to look up and feel that He is *yours,* and you are *His*—this is happiness.

You have sinned, perhaps very long and very greatly. But remember, "God is love" (1 John 4:8). He is full of mercy and ready to forgive. He has sent His dear Son to save sinners, and He will receive every penitent sinner who comes to Him through Christ, looking to His precious blood to save him.

Yes, dear friend, you may be very happy, happier in your old age than you have ever been before. God can give you happiness, and He *will* give it you, if you cast yourself on Him, and take Him as your portion.

Now, go to God and ask Him to show you your sins and to pardon them all for Jesus' sake. Oh, seek Him in earnest prayer, and never rest until you have found Him. Pray for the Holy Spirit. Entreat Him to come into your dark soul and enlighten it. Beseech Him to change your evil heart, to take away all that is wicked in it, and to fill it with what is holy and good. Ask Him to show Christ to you, and to enable you to believe in Him. Ask Him to lead you in the blessed path of holiness which He points out for His people. Then you will be happy. This is the grand secret of all peace. This gives rest for the weary soul, and joy for those who have never tasted it before.

But there are two or three more hints I would like to offer you.

Try to *take a bright view of everything*. Look at the sunny side of things. Do not dwell much on your pains and aches, your troubles and infirmities, your trials and misfortunes. They may be very great, but they will not grow lighter by always harping on them. Rather, love to dwell on your many blessings and your many mercies.

You will say perhaps, "I cannot help thinking of my troubles." But you can help it by making an effort to do so. A dull, complaining spirit grows upon people sometimes without their knowing it. Do try to check it, or it will make your days miserable and displeasing to God.

Determine to be *content with your lot*, whatever it is. Paul says, "I have learned" [and he found it a good lesson when he had learned it!] in whatsoever state I am, therewith to be content" (Phil. 4:11). A thankful and a contented spirit is a continual feast. We *ought* to be contented, and we *shall* be contented, if we are in the habit of seeing God in everything, and living upon Him day by day. Oh, for a spirit of true thankfulness!

Oh, for a heart to praise the Lord,

A heart from sin set free,
A heart that's sprinkled with the blood
So freely shed for me!

Jane Down was a woman of about sixty-five.
She was well off in the world, with a little money
of her own. I never went to see her when she did
not find something to complain about. Either
her head ached, or her knee troubled her, or
somebody had been speaking against her, or the
weather was too hot or too cold. You could at
once see that she had not found out the secret
of true happiness. She was a constant trouble to
herself and a weariness to her friends.

Widow Kingston lived near her. She was supported partly by her son, and partly by parish
pay. Her cottage was as clean and tidy as Jane
Down's, though she had not half as many things
in it. She was sure to welcome you with a smile
if you went to see her. She was sure to say something pleasant, and you felt afterwards that it did
you good to pay her a visit. She had not much of
this world's goods, but she possessed *Christ*. She
loved her Savior, and it was her greatest joy to
speak of His goodness. There was a calm peace in
that poor widow's heart, and nothing could rob
her of it. Having Christ, she had all.

What made the difference between these two
old people? What made the one contented and
happy, while the other was sour, discontented,
and miserable? It was grace that made them to

differ. The one was under the influence of the Holy Spirit; the other was destitute of His indwelling power. The one knew Christ and loved Him; to the other, He was a stranger.

Try to *live above the world.* A ship that is "homeward bound" cares little for the winds and waves as it sails on speedily towards the desired harbor. Heaven is the peaceful harbor you wish to reach. Then why think so much about the storms and tempests, which buffet you on your way? They will soon be over. Face them manfully. Take them patiently. Bear them meekly. Keep your eye ever fixed on Christ and eternity, and then the evils of this present world will not greatly trouble you.

Oh, that Christ may give you, dear reader, His own peace—the peace which He promised to His people when He said, "Peace I leave with you, my peace I give unto you: not as the world giveth, give I unto you" (John 14:27).

7

The Aged Christian
and His Bible

Possibly you have read a very nice tract called "The Shepherd of Salisbury Plain." This shepherd was a plain, simple man with scarcely any learning. But there was one sort of knowledge of which he had a great deal, and there was one kind of happiness which he enjoyed more than most men. He was one who feared and loved God, and the Holy Scriptures were his delight. He read them daily, and his soul was greatly refreshed and comforted by them. They were "more to him than his necessary food."

Some were astonished at his knowledge. They wondered how one who had had so little learning could know so much. Where did it come from? How was it, that he, a poor, uneducated man, had so much wisdom? He gleaned it all from the Word of God. That Word was brought home to his heart by the Holy Spirit, and it taught him much.

What has the Word of God done for *you*? Has it brought life and comfort to your soul? You have a Bible, I dare say, and often read it. But do you *enjoy* it? Is it precious to your soul? Would you rather give up every other book than give up your Bible? Is it your constant companion? Do you feel, as you read it, that it is as if *God* is speaking by it to your soul?

Two people may read their Bibles very differently. One may read a chapter or two every day, as regularly as the clock strikes. He may get through a vast deal of Scripture in the course of the year. The sacred volume may often be seen in his hand. Yet, he may be none the better for his reading. His mind may be as dark as ever, and his hopes of heaven as dim and cloudy. With all his reading, he may never receive God's truth into his soul. He may never know Christ as his Savior.

Another may study the Bible with far greater profit. He may not be a learned man, or have had much schooling. He may find a difficulty in making out some of the hard words he encounters. But he is a humble man, and so he looks up to God for *His* teaching. He never opens the Holy Volume without breathing a prayer—a secret, silent prayer, it may be, within his own heart—that the Holy Spirit may open his eyes and help him to understand and feel the truths he reads. Thus the Word falls like seed upon the open furrow. It does not remain on the surface, but sinks down into his very soul. It takes root there. It instructs him. It brings joy and peace to his heart. It makes him "wise unto salvation."

Let the Bible be your constant study. It is God's Word, and it is therefore the best of books. It tells you the way to be saved, therefore, it is most precious. It speaks to you of your Savior and your home, and therefore it should be most sweet to you.

I would recommend you to get a good, large Bible with a clear print. And when you have got it, lay great emphasis on it. Do not put it on the shelf and be afraid to use it for fear of its getting soiled. But read it very often, so that you may become well acquainted with its blessed truths. A happy thing it is, if you can say with one of old, "How sweet are thy words unto my taste! yea, sweeter than honey to my mouth" (Ps. 119:103).

I dare say you will find, in the course of your reading, much that you do not understand. Do not let this trouble you. There are many passages in God's Word which even the most learned find it difficult to explain. God's thoughts are higher than our thoughts, and His ways higher than our ways; it is no wonder that we cannot understand them.

I have heard of an aged Christian who was once asked, "How is it that you have so good a knowledge of your Bible?" "Why, this," she said, "is the plan I always use—when I come to a hard verse or a difficult word, I do not dwell much upon it; but I put a slip of paper in the page and then read on. And soon I come to some passage which explains the one I could not understand. Thus I am able to take out one marker after another. The consequence is that there are but few places which cause me much difficulty."

Try this plan, and I think you will find it works. There must be difficulties in God's Word, but Scripture will often explain Scripture. And, after all, ought we not to be very thankful that there is so much that we *can* understand, so much that we can receive for the life and nourishment of our souls?

One thing is very necessary, and that is to read the Bible with prayer. Our minds are dark and ignorant, and we need enlightening. Now, even if we had a friend always at our elbow, ready to explain to us every passage, we should still need something more, for man cannot make the blind eye to see. This is God's work. He who commanded the light to shine out of darkness— He who said, "Let there be light, and there was light," must shine into our hearts.

Then ask for His enlightening grace. Pray earnestly that the Holy Spirit may come and dwell within you. He is the teacher that we want, for "who teacheth like him?"

Whenever you open the Bible, remember to ask God to open your heart. Put up some short and simple prayer as this: "O Lord, I am blind and ignorant; do Thou enlighten me. Teach me by Thy Holy Spirit; and grant that Thy Word may do my soul good, for Christ's sake."

There are few prayers more fitting for this purpose than that short but beautiful prayer which is in the Anglican Book of Prayer. Let us see that we understand it. "Blessed Lord, who hast caused all Holy Scriptures to be written for our learning"—here we acknowledge that the Scriptures are God's Word, which He has made men to write expressly for our instruction. "Grant that we may in such wise hear them, read, mark, learn, and inwardly digest them"—here is a prayer that we may not only read the words with our eyes, but that we may dwell upon them; gather from them something for our good; and turn them over and over in our minds, just as animals chew the food they eat, in order to digest it. "That by patience and comfort of Thy Holy Word, we may embrace, and ever hold fast, the blessed hope of everlasting life, which Thou hast given us in our Savior Jesus Christ." This is the great object of reading God's Word—that we may get comfort from it, and be enabled to lay fast hold of that everlasting life which Christ has purchased to us.

You see there is a great deal in this prayer, and it is very suitable to our wants. But it matters not whether you use the prayer I have mentioned, or any other suitable words, so long as you earnestly pray for God's teaching and blessing.

If you read the Bible in a prayerful, humble, childlike spirit, I am sure you will not read it in vain. You will find there a treasure, which will enrich and comfort your soul day by day.

There was a time when the Bible was a scarce and expensive book, so that few could possess it. Now, thank God, it can be purchased by the poorest person, and we may each have a copy of it to call our own. May we prize it as our dearest possession, and be very thankful to God for giving us so rich a gift!

Holy Bible! Book Divine!
Precious treasure, thou art mine;
Mine, to tell me whence I came;
Mine, to teach me what I am;

Mine, to chide me when I rove;
Mine, to show a Savior's love;
Mine art thou to guide my feet;
Mine, to judge, condemn, acquit;

Mine, to comfort in distress,
If the Holy Spirit bless;
Mine, to show by living faith,
Man can triumph over death;

Mine to tell of joys to come,
And the rebel sinner's doom.
Oh thou precious book divine!
Precious treasure, thou art mine!

8

The Aged Christian in the House of God

The house of God has special charms for the Christian in his old age. There is a calm, quiet, soul-refreshing atmosphere there, which is peculiarly sweet to one who longs for rest. You can leave the noise and turmoil of the world, with all its vanities and sins, and there meet your God, and hold sweet communion with Him.

The Lord is everywhere. He is about our path, and about our bed. But He is especially with us in His own house. There we feel His nearness, and we are sometimes ready to exclaim, as Jacob did at Bethel, "Surely the Lord is in this place.... This is none other but the house of God, and this is the gate of heaven" (Gen. 28:16-17).

Good old Eli loved the Lord's house. Many a happy and blessed hour he spent in those sacred courts. David too rejoiced to be there: "A day in thy courts is better than a thousand [spent elsewhere]. I had rather be a doorkeeper in the house of my God, than to dwell in the tents of wicked-

ness" (Ps. 84:10). Simeon enjoyed his visits to
the temple. There it was that he saw the Savior,
whom he so greatly longed to behold. And this
made him quite willing to die: "Lord, now lettest
thou thy servant depart in peace, according to
thy word: for mine eyes have seen thy salvation"
(Luke 2:29-30). We read also in the gospels
of Anna, who was "of a great age...a widow of
about fourscore and four years, which departed
not from the temple, but served God with fast-
ings and prayers night and day" (Luke 2:36-37).
The house of God was her delight. It seemed like
a little heaven below. The voice of prayer and
praise was music in her ears.

Well, dear brother or sister, I hope *you* can say
of the courts of the Lord, "I love to be there. There
I have spent my happiest moments. There I have
found a peace of which the world can never rob
me. There I have often had my heart warmed with
love to Christ and to His people. There I have
oftentimes gone with a heavy burden; but I have
left it behind me, and come away lightened."

Dear is to me the Sabbath morn,
The village bells, the pastor's voice,
These oft have found my heart forlorn,
And these have bid my heart rejoice.

And dear to me the winged hour,
Spent in Thy hallowed courts, O Lord;
To feel devotion's soothing power,
And catch the manna of Thy Word.

And dear to me the loud Amen,
Which echoes through the blest abode,
Which swells and sinks, and swells again,
Dies on the walls, but lives to God.

Oh, when the world, with iron hand,
Would bind me in its six days' chain,
Thus burst, O Lord, the strong man's band,
And let my spirit loose again.

But it is not every kind of church attendance that does us good. Many a young person, and many an old one, too, goes without getting much profit. Let me offer you then a few friendly directions.

1. Always go to God's house *expecting a blessing.* Look for it, and especially ask for it. Go in a devout spirit. Before you leave your home, kneel down for a moment or two and beg of the Lord to prepare your heart by His Holy Spirit and enable you to worship Him as you ought.

2. When there, *enter with all your heart into the service.* During the prayers, join earnestly with your fellow-worshippers. It is not enough to sit quietly while your minister sends up his petitions to heaven; but *pray the prayers yourself.* Yes, pray them with all your soul.

3. When the lessons are read out of God's Word, *listen with your whole attention.* It may be you have

often heard those chapters before, or read them yourself; but they contain precious truths, which are always new to the hearing ear and the understanding heart.

4. During the sermon, *be a humble listener*. You should be as a little child, feeling that your knowledge is but small, and that you have much to learn. You should be like a hungry man who comes to be fed, seeking to get your soul nourished by the bread of life. You should be like the thirsty soil, which waits to drink in the falling shower. If we all heard in this way, who can tell what blessings would flow from every service, and how many would come away from this ordinance of God filled and refreshed?

Perhaps you are growing deaf, and can only pick up a part of what is said by the preacher. Perhaps, too, your memory fails you when you try to gather up what you have heard. Still, you can carry away *something*, and you will be thankful for that something if you feel that it is a part of God's own message.

5. Another direction I will give you. When you come home from church, *do not forget the service in which you have been engaging*. Converse about it, if you have an opportunity. Get out your Bible, and find the text; and then talk over any part of the sermon which you can remember. This is the way to refresh your memory, and to lay up a store of spiritual knowledge.

6. When Holy Communion is administered, do not fail to receive it. Be thankful when your Communion Sundays come around, and rejoice in the opportunity of feeding on the body and blood of Christ.

Some old persons "take the sacrament," as they call it, as a mere matter of form. They come to the Lord's Table because there is something respectable in doing so, or because their minister expects to see them there. But if they only come for this reason, it is to them but a poor, cold, dry, unmeaning service, and, instead of pleasing God, they only offend Him.

But I trust that you, my dear friend, are not one of these formal communicants. I trust that you come to this blessed ordinance under a deep feeling of your own sinfulness and unworthiness, and desire to draw near to Christ with humble and living faith. You come, not because you are worthy to come, but because you feel your need for strength and grace. You come to Jesus to be pardoned and healed, and to receive fresh life from Him.

I have said that David and Simeon and Eli and Anna loved God's house. But you have reason to love it even more than they did, for they lived only in Jewish days. The light was but very dim then. But now it shines brightly and clearly upon us. Christ is come, and He is plainly set before us as "the way, the truth, and the life" (John 14:6).

Then love the house of God. Go there as often as the bells of the sanctuary call you. And remember your Savior's gracious promise: "Where two or three are gathered together in my name, there am I in the midst of them" (Matt. 18:20).

May your Sabbaths be more and more happy as you draw nearer to that endless Sabbath which you hope to spend above! May your love for God's day, for God's house, for God's Word, and for God's people be ever increasing until you are called away to join the one family in heaven, and sit down with Abraham, Isaac, and Jacob in the kingdom of God!

Thine earthly Sabbaths, Lord, I love,
But there's a nobler rest above.
Oh that I might that rest attain,
From sin, from sorrow, and from pain!

~9~

The Aged Christian
in His Closet

There are times when we need to be alone with God. There are times when the Christian wants to get away from others, and draw near to his heavenly Father. Our Lord knew that this was needful for the well-being of our souls; and therefore He said, "Thou, when thou prayest, *enter into thy closet,* and when thou hast *shut thy door,* pray to thy Father which is *in secret*" (Matt. 6:6). Jesus, you see, is here speaking of private prayer, when no one is present with us but God Himself.

Think about *how great your need is,* as regards both your body and your soul. Have you no need of God's protecting care to keep you alive from day to day? Have you no need of His guiding hand to direct you in your path? Have you no need of His grace to keep you from falling into sin, and to strengthen your faith? Have you no bad habits to get rid of, and no bad tempers to subdue? Are there no friends or neighbors for whom you should intercede? Is there no work of Christ going on in the world, for which you should pray? Surely these are matters which are very important for you to bring before God.

Think, too, *how great are your sins*. There are sins, committed long ago in the days of your youth, for which you need pardon. And there are later sins, newly committed perhaps, which lie heavy on your conscience; these too must be forgiven, or you cannot be happy. Oh, how many things there are which we have left undone, how many that we have done wrongly, how many little sins which we scarcely notice at the time, how many secret sins which the world knows nothing of! We must carry all these to the cross, and entreat Christ to wash them away in His own blood.

Think again *how great are your mercies*. You have cause to thank your heavenly Father for all His past goodness to you, and for all His present gifts. Oh, how great they are, and how little you have deserved them! Why has He spared you so long? Why are you yet alive, when so many have been cut off? Has He not fed you and clothed you all your life long? Has He not preserved you from ten thousand dangers? Has He not shielded you in the hour of temptation? Has He not kept you from sin, when others have fallen into it?

A clergyman was once visiting a hospital. As he went from bed to bed in the different wards, he came to an old man, who was apparently suffering much pain. He began to express his pity for this poor sufferer. "Is there anything, my friend, that you want?" he asked. "No," replied the old man; "I have many mercies and blessings in this place. I want but one thing." "And what is that?" asked the clergyman. "I want," said he, "a more thankful heart."

Yes, we have all of us great *needs*, great *sins*, and great *mercies*. And this should bring us on our knees and stir us up to prayer.

But, my dear friend, do you know what prayer, *real* prayer, is? It is not the mere utterance of words. It is not the mere moving of the lips. It is not the mere repeating of a string of sentences which we have learned by heart. No, this is not prayer. Prayer is drawing near to our gracious Father, telling Him all about our soul, begging of Him to pardon all our sins, asking Him to give us all we need, and thanking Him for His daily mercies. Prayer is speaking to God, though we cannot see Him.

You need not offer up *long* prayers. God does not judge them by their length, but He looks at our earnestness. You need not offer up *learned* prayers. The sighing of a contrite heart and the words of a soul that *feels* are enough for Him. Perhaps you find it best to speak to God in your own words, or perhaps you had rather use some written prayer. It matters little which, only that your prayer comes from the heart.

Let me now say a word as to *when* you should offer up prayer. Certainly morning and evening

are the natural times for such a service. I dare
say you have always been accustomed to say your
prayers then. We should begin and end the day
upon our knees. We should do nothing in the
morning before we have solemnly put ourselves
under God's care; and in the evening one of our
last acts should be to visit the throne of grace
before we lie down to rest. Yes, these are the two
best and most proper seasons for regular prayer.

But, dear friend, if you know the value of
prayer, you will not be content with your morning and evening devotions. Twelve or fourteen
hours are a long while to go without speaking to
your heavenly Friend. I would recommend you
to have a little time for prayer *in the middle of the
day*. Get a quiet five or ten minutes if you can at
noon. This was David's custom and Daniel's; it
is the custom of most of God's people. I strongly
advise you to try it, if you have not already done
so. When you come to die, you will not feel that
you have prayed too much or too often. Your sorrow will then be that, although God was always
ready to hear you, you were so backward in drawing near to Him.

But does not Paul say, "Pray *without ceasing*"
(1 Thes. 5:17)? This, at first sight, seems to be a
very hard direction to follow. To be always praying! To be ever on our knees! To be at the throne
of grace all the day long! This is more than the
holiest men, even Paul himself, could do. What
he means, I think, is that we should be always *in*

a praying frame, that we should be ready to go to Him on all occasions, and that there should be a constant communion between us and our God.

Try then to act on Paul's advice. Besides praying at stated times, get into the habit of putting up a word or two to God *often* during the day. When you are sitting in your chair, you can lift up your heart to God. When you are walking along the street, you can breathe out a secret petition to your gracious Father. Though you say nothing aloud, your inward soul can pray. No one may be listening to you; but God, who heareth in secret, hearkens to your request.

For instance, if you are going to do anything for which you need strength given to you, put up some such words as these, "Lord, help me." If a feeling of your sinfulness comes across you, you may breathe a secret prayer, saying, "Lord, save me." Or if you want to have your Savior near you, you may dart up some such short request as this, "O Lord, be with me; Jesus, make me to feel Thy presence."

My dear reader, if you wish to live a heavenly life, this habit will be a great help to you. It will keep you close to God and will bring down His grace upon you. If you are a true Christian, you will love prayer, especially now that your praying time will soon be over.

You hope to spend eternity with God; oh, then seek to know Him and to love Him *now*. Let Him be no stranger to you, but your daily and hourly companion. If you had a friend near you whom you especially loved, should you not wish often to look upon him? Should you not feel that those moments that you spent in his presence were the happiest, when he was by your side? Should you not be often speaking to him? I am sure you would. Then act the same with Him who is better than all earthly friends, in whose favor is life, and whose presence is fullness of joy.

If you wish to be much blest, pray. If you wish to have a foretaste of heaven even while on earth, pray. If you wish to know, and to love, and to possess Christ, be much in prayer. If you wish to tread safely the path of life, and to go on your way rejoicing, pray, "Pray without ceasing." "In everything by prayer and supplication with thanksgiving let your requests be made known unto God" (Phil. 4:6).

~10~

The Aged Christian Ready
for His Departure

One would think that the longer a person lived, the more willing he would be to leave his present abode. But this is not always the case.

Sometimes, alas, we see very aged persons clinging to life more tightly than even the young. We see them close to the grave's mouth, and yet loving the riches, the pleasures, and the trifles of this world with all their affections. Oh, this is a sad sight. It is sad to see a poor, dying creature entering upon an awful eternity, with a heart glued to the world which he is leaving, and full of its concerns! When this is the case, God often in mercy sends us some affliction. He withers our gourds which have grown up around us, that He may lead us to seek a truer and a safer shelter. He sees that we are too fond of these clay cottages of ours, and He makes the walls crumble so that we will be content to leave them at His call.

Look at your growing infirmities, dear reader, as so many mercies. Let them serve to remind you that you will not be here always, and that "this is not your rest" (Micah 2:10). Let them make you long for that happier land, where there shall be no more old age, where sorrow and sighing shall be unknown, and where the inhabitant shall not say, "I am sick." Oh, it is well for us that all is not health and strength and sunshine here; else we should be even more fond than we are of our present home. I do not ask you to take a gloomy view of this world, and to be full of anxiety to leave it. I do not wish you to look upon it as a dungeon from which you are impatiently longing to escape. No; while we are here, we should be thankful. We should look upon it not as our lasting home, but as our appointed dwelling-place for awhile. It is well if we are contented and happy here, and at the same time ever ready for our departure. Well is it indeed, if we can say with Paul, as this world closes in upon us, "I am now ready to be offered, and the time of my departure is at hand. I have fought a good fight, I have finished my course, I have kept the faith: Henceforth there is laid up for me a crown of righteousness" (2 Tim. 4:6-8).

Sit as loose then as you can with regard to this world, and be always in a state of readiness to leave it. Arrange all your worldly concerns. The more cares you have upon your hands, the more will your dying thoughts be disturbed and your last work interrupted. Our deathbed moments are solemn ones; therefore, it is very desirable to have nothing to do then but to die.

Above all, let not the work of salvation be left undone. Every funeral you see or hear of, every pain and infirmity you feel seems to say to you, as Isaiah said to Hezekiah, "Set thy house in order" (Isa. 38:1). It is a poor thing to leave for last the soul's great work. It is often too late to seek a Savior then. The body will then perhaps be too weak, and the mind too feeble, to begin to seek the Lord. Perhaps too the Savior, when we most need Him, will then be far off from us. Having rejected Him, He will turn His face away from us, and leave us to ourselves in that trying hour. Oh then, "seek ye the Lord, while he may be found; call upon him *while he is near*" (Isa. 55:6).

There are many old people, who, if you question them about the future, will say that they *hope* all will be well. But if you press your question a little more closely, you will find that perhaps they have *no ground* for their hope. They trust that God will be merciful to them; but they cannot say with the apostle, "I *have obtained* mercy." They have never sought it in Christ, where alone it is to be found. They have never fled for refuge to the Savior. They love Him a little, but they have not given Him their heart. All is uncertain with them. This world is slipping from under them, and they have no sure footing on the heavenly shore.

It is a fearful thing to take the last and most important steps of our journey alone and in the dark, not knowing where we are going, whether to heaven or hell, not sure whether we have the friendship of God or not. Dear friend, it must not be so with you, or your deathbed will be a cheerless one.

Suppose someone was going to take a long journey; he ought to be ready for it. His traveling clothes should be prepared. Nothing should be left unsettled. Everything should be put in order. He ought to know all about the way that he is going to take. He ought to have no misgivings about his journey. His mind should be quite made up.

Should we be less ready for that great and important step which we are all going to take? Our happiness—our eternal safety—depends on it. Oh, that we may be able to say, "I die daily"; "the world is crucified unto me, and I unto the world" (Gal. 6:14); "To me to live is Christ; to die is gain" (Phil. 1:21). Live as a stranger and a pilgrim upon earth; look forward daily to your home, and be hastening towards it. Live much with Christ now; and then, instead of dreading death, you will heartily welcome it when it comes. You will not look upon it as your foe but as your friend. It will be to you as the gateway through which you will pass to your joyful resurrection. You will feel no lingering attachment to the world you are leaving behind you, but you will have "a desire to depart, and to be with Christ, which is far better" (Phil. 1:23).

Heavenly Mansion

I have a home above,
  From sin and sorrow free,
A mansion which eternal Love
  Designed and formed for me.
  My Father's gracious hand
  Has built this sweet abode;
From everlasting it was planned,
  My dwelling-place with God.

  My Savior's precious blood
  Has made my title sure;
He passed through death's dark raging flood,
  To make my rest secure.
  The Comforter is come,
  The promise has been given
He leads me onward to the home
  Reserved for me in Heaven.

  Bright angels guard my way,
  His ministers of power,
Encamping round me night and day,
  Keep me in danger's hour.
  Loved ones are gone before,
  Whose pilgrim days are done:
I soon shall meet them on that shore
  Where partings are unknown.

  Thy love, Thou precious Lord,
  My joy and strength shall be,
Till Thou shalt speak the gladdening word
  That bids me rise to Thee.
  And then through endless days,
  Where all Thy glories shine,
In happier, holier strains I'll praise
  The grace that made me Thine.

The Aged Christian
in Death

Death sometimes seizes the young. Sometimes it overtakes a person as he journeys carelessly along the road of life. Sometimes it checks the seed before it springs up. Sometimes it nips the flower as it begins to open to the sun.

But death, while it has seized one and another, has hitherto passed you by. You have lived, it may be, your three or fourscore years. But now your turn is coming. The shore of eternity is not far off. You feel that you are drawing near to it.

Perhaps death has sounded its warning note in your ear. Its chariot wheels are drawing near. Your strength is breaking up. Your appetite is gone. Your hearing is dull. Your sight has grown dim. Ah, if this were your only home, it would be a sad one now. If your only delights were to be found in the world, your lot would indeed be a mournful one, for the world can do but little for you in your present state. It seems to turn its back upon you now.

But take courage. Your heavenly Father is near. He has blessings for you. He will not leave you in your declining years. "Even to your old age I am he; and even to hoar hairs will I carry you" (Isa. 46:4). He is able to strengthen and comfort you in your hour of weakness. He can give you a peace which the world never gave you.

Now, I dare say you wish to die well. You wish to leave this world with a good hope, do you not? Then three things are especially necessary to make your deathbed a happy one.

1. You must be brought to *feel your guilt* in God's sight. Many acknowledge this *in words*, but they do not thoroughly feel it *in their hearts*. But if the Holy Spirit awakens your soul, if you are really brought under His blessed influence, then you will not merely *speak* of being a sinner; you will *feel*, and that deeply, the burden and guilt of sin. What a difference there is between the cold acknowledgment that *you and all the world* have sinned, and that deep conviction of sin which leads you to cry out in the agony of your soul, "God be merciful to *me* a sinner!"

Ask God to make you see what sin is. Pray that the Holy Spirit will show you your guilt, and lead you to sigh and cry for its removal.

"Ah," you will say, "is *this* what you mean by happiness on a deathbed? Such thoughts as these will only make me miserable." There is some truth in this. But depend upon it, there can be no real happiness until you have felt your misery and had it removed. Your wound must be probed and laid open before it can be healed. And is not this a *blessed* misery, if it leads to happiness? What if sorrow endures for a night, so long as joy dawns upon us in the morning? It is better to feel your sins *now*, than to feel them when you are *beyond the reach of pardoning mercy*. I always think that those are on the fair road to happiness who have made the discovery that they have wandered and strayed from the right way, and are earnestly seeking to find a better path.

Look closely into your own evil heart. Try and bring every sin from its hiding-place. Some of them lie very deep. Pray then, "Search me, O God, and know my heart: try me, and know my thoughts: and see if there be any wicked way in me, and lead me in the way everlasting" (Ps. 139:23-24).

Remember that there is not a sin which you have ever been guilty of, even though it be years and years ago, that is not written down in God's memory. The sins of your youth, which you may have long since quite forgotten—there they are, as fresh as if they had just been committed. Yes, you need to ask God to wipe them out of His remembrance, though they will continue fresh in *your own*. The prayer of David will just suit you, "Remember not the sins of my youth, nor my transgressions: according to thy mercy remember thou me for thy goodness' sake, O LORD" (Ps. 25:7).

To feel your sins then is important, very important. But something more is needed. You must get them *pardoned, blotted out, put away for ever.* And how can this be?

2. There is a way by which the guiltiest may obtain *forgiveness.* There is a fountain in which the vilest may wash and be clean. The blood of Christ can wipe away our deepest stains. God has sent His Son to die upon the cross, and in that cross you may find mercy.

But perhaps you fancy that you have no great need of such a Savior—that you have done nothing particularly wrong, that your heart is as clean as others', that you have lived a tolerably harmless life, and that God will at last accept you? No, dear friend, you are a sinner, a great sinner, in God's sight, though man may have nothing to lay to your charge. Oh, how much you have left undone! How much you have done wrongly! How much you have thought about your body, and how little about your soul! How much have you cared about this world, and how little about that which is coming! How much more have you loved yourself and your children than you have loved your Lord!

Be assured your sins are great and many—far greater, and far more in number, than you can blot out. Go then, and cast yourself on Christ the great Sin-bearer. Bring your debt to Him, who has paid it with His blood. Believe on Him. Give your whole heart to Him. Say, "Lord, enable me to love Thee. Make me to taste of Thy preciousness. Look upon me, a vile sinner. Help me in my great need. Pardon all my guilt, and clothe me with Thy perfect righteousness."

3. But further, we need *a holy heart*. God must give this. He can take away "the heart of stone," the hard, unbelieving, unloving heart; He can give you a "heart of flesh," a believing, loving, tender heart. Happy are those in whom the Holy Spirit dwells, whose souls are filled with His grace, and are daily more and more conformed to the image and likeness of Christ.

Can we ever be *perfectly and completely* holy here? No, we shall carry about with us a sinful nature to the very last. Our refuge in a dying hour must not be any goodness of our own, but the merits and atonement of Jesus our Savior.

Perhaps these words may fall into the hands of one who has been long lying upon a sick-bed. Dear reader, your bed *may* be a bed of peace, and it *will* be so if you have found a Savior. All is well if God is your God, and Christ your Savior. Then you need not fear. He who is your Father keeps you there. You are *His* prisoner. He has the keys, and in His own good time He will unlock the door, and welcome you into His presence, to be with Him for ever.

Or perhaps your end is near. Happy is it for you, if death and eternity are no strangers to you. Happy for you, if Jesus is your portion, and heaven your home. Then you have only to die a death which has lost its sting. Christ has plucked it out. You can say with the apostle, "I know whom I have believed." And you can add with David, "Though I walk through the valley of the shadow of death, I will fear no evil: for thou art with me; thy rod and thy staff they comfort me" (Ps. 23:4).

There is now but a step between you and death. And well that it is so, if you are a true servant of God. You have nothing to dread. Death, which is "the king of terrors" to the ungodly, shall be a welcome messenger to you. It is like the plank on which the sailor walks to shore, after having been tossed on the troubled ocean. It will bear you to your Father's arms. It will lay you in your Savior's bosom.

Ah, though it is hard to bear weakness and suffering, though days of pain and nights of weariness are appointed you, still you will willingly endure all this if Christ is with you. If He "makes all your bed in your sickness," then that bed will be a bed of blessing to you. It is better to lie there with God for your friend than to enjoy health and strength without Him. Your last illness may be a very precious time to you, the most important season of your whole life, the time when you shall receive the fullest communications from God, and enjoy the truest peace.

Let Christ be your watchword in death, your hope, your joy, your portion, your all. Think of Him, when you can think of nothing else. Cling to Him, when all else is slipping as it were from under you. Be assured, He will never leave you, nor forsake you.

I have read of a dying Christian, a venerable servant of God, whose wife and children stood around his bed weeping. His speech was almost gone, and his memory had nearly left him. One of his children had asked him, "Father, do you remember me?" and received no answer. Another and another also, but still no answer. Then his aged partner drew near. She bent over him; as tears fell down her cheeks, she said, "Do you not remember me?" A stare—but it is a vacant stare. There was no light in that filmy eye. The seal of death was upon those lips. His sun had almost gone down. The shadows of death were upon him.

Then one calmer than the rest, who remembered that the love of Christ is "strong as death," stooped to his ear, and said, "Do you remember *Christ*?" That name seemed for a moment to call back his consciousness. His pale countenance lighted up like the last beam of day, and with a smile he replied, "Remember Christ! Dear Christ! He is all my salvation, and all my desire."

May this be your feeling and mine in the hour of our departure!

Guide me, O Thou great Jehovah!
Pilgrim through this barren land;
I am weak, but Thou art mighty;
Hold me with Thy powerful hand;
    Bread of heaven,
    Feed me now and evermore.

Open Thou the crystal fountain,
When the healing streams do flow;
Let the fiery, cloudy pillar
Lead me all my journey through;
    Strong Deliverer,
    Be Thou still my strength and shield.

When I tread the verge of Jordan,
Bid my anxious fears subside;
Death of deaths, and hell's destruction,
Land me safe on Canaan's side;
    Songs of praises,
    I will ever give to Thee.

— W. Williams

~12~

The Aged Christian
in Heaven

What is heaven? Where is it? We know not. And there are many more questions we should like to ask about it, but they cannot be answered. This, however, we know—heaven is a *holy* place, a *happy* place, an eternal *resting*-place, the abode of God Himself.

It is a holy place. The Word of God says, "There shall in no wise enter into it anything that defileth" (Rev. 21:27). No unpardoned one shall be there, no Christless souls, none with unchanged hearts.

This world is under a curse. Sin spoils all our actions. But there will be "no more curse" in heaven. We shall be holy as the angels. We shall be like the Savior. "Beloved," says John, "now are we the sons of God, and it doth not yet appear what we shall be: but we know that, when he shall appear, we shall be like him" (1 John 3:2).

Heaven will be a *happy* place, too. Where there is holiness there must be happiness. When is it that we enjoy the most peace here? Is it not when we are living nearest to God, doing His will, and following Him faithfully? Think then how great will be our bliss in heaven, when we shall be holy as He is holy.

There will be nothing to interfere with our joy then. One would think that our happiness would be spoiled by the absence of some whom we loved here on earth, and who will not be there to share our heaven with us. But no; in some way God will prevent even this from grieving us. So long as He is glorified, we shall be content. Our song will be, "Just and true are thy ways, thou King of saints" (Rev. 15:3).

I hope you can feel that you have many happy moments now. But every moment will be happy in heaven. Now it is only checkered happiness; sorrow creeps in. But then it will be perfect and unmixed. Now you feel peace, when you think of Jesus, and what He has done for you; when your cold heart is warmed with His love, you are happy. But then your heart will be *filled full* of His love, and your cup of joy will run over.

Heaven is an *everlasting resting-place*. Oh, what a world of toil and trial this is! Perhaps you have had to work hard all your life, and eat your bread with labor. Perhaps you have also lived hard, and often found a difficulty in getting enough. You have met with many a trial in your day, and this has left its mark on your care-worn brow. But there will be an end of all this in heaven. It has been said, "Earth for toil; heaven for repose." There the weary rest. The tired limbs will ache no more. The tear will not again trickle down your cheek. There will be no more strife and confusion. We shall be no more tossed about on the troublesome waves of this world. All will be rest.

But it will not be a rest of sloth and idleness. There would be no happiness in that. We shall all serve God day and night. The angels serve Him now; it is their greatest joy to be employed for Him. And so it will be with us. To do His will will be our constant employment, and to sing His praises our great delight. We shall not rest day nor night, saying, "Holy, holy, holy, Lord God Almighty."

Heaven is the *dwelling-place of God Himself.* We shall be with Him. We shall spend eternity in His presence. What an honor! What blessedness! If we have any dear friend on earth whom we especially love, are we not very happy in his company? What will it be to be near our Lord—to see Him, and be with Him, forever? "Behold, the tabernacle of God is with men, and he will dwell with them, and they shall be his people, and *God himself shall be with them*" (Rev. 21:3).

This, my dear friend, is the prospect before you. Why should you grieve then that your earthly house is tottering and giving way, when you have such a house as this in store for you? Oh, be of good courage. A few more days in this weary world, and then a home of joy for ever!

Is this home yours? I hope it is. Jesus has prepared it for sinners like you. But remember, you need to be prepared for it. You need to have every sin washed away in your Savior's blood. You have an evil, wicked heart. Ask God to take it away, and to give you a new and clean heart. Ask the Holy Spirit to teach you, to enlighten you, to show Christ to you, and to make you every day more and more like your Savior. Ask Him to bend your will to His.

It is possible that some reader of these pages may have been traveling all his life long *towards hell*. He may have followed his own ways and despised the ways of God. He may have loved sin and rejected the Savior. And now he has come to the brink of eternity; all before him is dark and hopeless.

Oh sinner, I tremble for you. It is written, "The wicked shall be turned *into hell*, and all the nations that forget God" (Ps. 9:17). "The wages of sin is *death*" (Rom. 6:23). What is to become of you? You will soon die. And what then? What is there after death? There is the awful judgment, the great white throne, and all gathered before it, and you among the number. The books will be opened, and your sins all written there! And then the *sentence*—the just and righteous *sentence!* Oh, who shall stand when He appeareth? Who shall dwell with everlasting burnings?

Your case is bad, very bad. Shall I say that it is utterly hopeless? No, I dare not say so. I have seen, on a dark, gloomy day when almost the whole heavens have been covered with a thick mantle of clouds, a little speck of light in the distant sky, which has given me hope. And if you open God's Word, you may see a little bright opening of hope ever nigh. There is a whisper from heaven to you, more welcome than the gleam of sunshine, which says, "Come now, and let us reason together, saith the Lord: though your sins be as scarlet, they shall be as white as snow; though they be red like crimson, they shall be as wool" (Isa. 1:18).

You have greatly sinned. You have done much to shut yourself out from God's mercy. But He has followed you in all your wanderings. He is ready to win you back. He calls to you in words of love and tenderness. He seems now *once more* to hold the door of mercy open. He seems to say to you, "Why will ye die?" He can pardon *even now*. Think of the cross. Throw yourself down, as it were, before it. Look there for mercy, and *you may yet find it.*

Yes, my brother, or my sister, you are late, very late; but your day of grace is not yet past. You may seek Christ, and find Him even now.

"Today, if ye will hear his voice, harden not your hearts" (Heb. 3:15).

But if, on the other hand, you are a true servant of Christ, though you feel yourself unworthy to be called His—if, as you have grown in years, you have gone on loving and serving Him more and more—then you may think of death without alarm; and what is more, you may think of the bright and happy *home beyond.*

Is there not something very sweet in those words, "my home"? Happy the hardworking laborer, who, when evening comes, has a home to return to! Happy the prisoner, who, when his day of liberty arrives, has a home to receive him! Happy the traveler, who journeys on with the cheering prospect that he is getting nearer home! But still more happy the Christian, whether rich or poor, who, after a long life in this changing world, has a sure and certain hope that he is daily and hourly drawing nearer to his heavenly home! And how sweet the thought of entering that home, never more to leave it! How blessed, when all our trials and all our journeyings are over, to enjoy that rest which remaineth to the people of God! Then we shall be permitted to sing:

> *It is no longer "going home,"*
> *For heaven is reached at last;*
> *The weary wilderness, thank God,*
> *Is now for ever passed.*

I've bid the world a glad farewell;
I've done with suffering now;
And never more one passing grief
Shall shade my peaceful brow.

I've reached at length my native land,
The place I truly love:
Clad in my Savior's spotless robe,
I've joined the hosts above.

I've reached my home, that home so dear
To every pilgrim's heart;
And never shall my feet again
From its glad walls depart.

I've joined that blessed band above
Of brethren kindred dear;
But better far, my Lord I see,
And His loved voice I hear.

I've reached my home, my happy home,
So holy and so pure;
And (blessed thought!) I know it shall
Eternally endure.

For those whom Jesus died to save,
He ever lives to bless;
Those mansions which His love prepares,
His children shall possess.

And now, dear reader, it is time that I bid you

farewell. If I have said one word that has helped you on your way, if you have learned a single truth from this book, if I have given a little spur to your faith, or kindled a spark of love in your soul—if, in short, you are in any way the better for having read these pages—to God be all the praise! We shall both give it to Him throughout eternity.

May you and I, unworthy as we are, be numbered among God's blood-bought family, among the Savior's friends! And may we hereafter sit down together in the kingdom of our Father!

Hymns for the Aged

For a Time of Sickness

When languor and disease invade
    This trembling house of clay,
'Tis sweet to look beyond our cage,
    And long to fly away.

Sweet to look inward and attend
    The whispers of His love;
Sweet to look upward to the place
    Where Jesus pleads above.

Sweet to look back, and see my name
    In life's fair book set down;
Sweet to look forward, and behold
    Eternal joys my own.

Sweet to reflect how grace divine
    My sins on Jesus laid;
Sweet to remember that His blood
    My debt of suffering paid.

Sweet in His righteousness to stand,
    Which saves from second death;
Sweet to experience day by day
    His Spirit's guiding breath.

Sweet in His faithfulness to rest,
    Whose love can never end;
Sweet on His covenant of grace
    For all things to depend.

Sweet in the confidence of faith
    To trust His firm decrees;
Sweet to lie passive in His hands,
    And know no will but His.

If such the sweetness of the stream
    What must the fountain be,
Where saints and angels draw their bliss
    Immediately from Thee?

                — A. Toplady

The Pilgrim's Song

A pilgrim and a stranger,
I journey here below;
Far distant is my country,
The Home to which I go.
Here I must toil and travel,
Oft weary and oppressed,
But there my God shall lead me
To everlasting rest.

I've met with storms and dangers
E'en from my early years,
With enemies and conflicts,
With fightings and with fears.

There's nothing here that tempts me
To wish a longer stay;
So I must hasten forwards,
No halting or delay.

So I must hasten forwards,
Thank God the end will come!
The land of my sojourning
Is not my destined home;
That evermore abideth,
Jerusalem above,
The everlasting city,
The land of light and love.

There still my thoughts are dwelling;
'Tis there I long to be
Come, Lord, and call Thy servant
To blessedness with Thee.
Come, bid my toils be ended,
Let all my wand'rings cease,
Call from the wayside lodging
To the sweet home of peace.

There I shall dwell for ever,
No more a stranger guest,
With all Thy blood-bought children
In everlasting rest.
The pilgrim toils forgotten,
The pilgrim conflicts o'er,
All earthly griefs behind us,
Eternal joys before.

Submission

My God and Father, while I stray
Far from my home on life's rough way,
Oh, teach me from my heart to say,
    "Thy will be done."

If Thou dost call me to resign
What most I prize—it ne'er was mine;
I only yield Thee what was Thine:
    "Thy will be done."

Should pining sickness waste away
My life in premature decay,
My Father, still I strive to say,
    "Thy will be done."

If but my fainting heart be blest
With Thy sweet Spirit for my guest,
My God, to Thee I leave the rest:
    "Thy will be done."

Renew my will from day to day;
Blend it with Thine, and take away
All that now makes it hard to say,
    "Thy will be done."

Then, when on earth I breathe no more,
The prayer, oft mixed with tears before
I'll sing upon a happier shore,
    "Thy will be done."